VEGAN POWER!
(The Compassionate Mind)

Andrew J Jones

Copyright 2015
Owned by Andrew J Jones.

Table of Contents

Acknowledgements.....5
Introduction.....6

Questions From The Foolish Flock.....7
I Don't Want to Die.....11
Marcia Oldfield.....12
Hell on Earth.....14
Tracy Joy Aplin.....17
Your Children.....19
Jahara Rhiannon.....21
Aisha Sulayman.....22
Nathan Budda Bowcott.....22
Martyn Jones.....22
Martin Caviel.....23
Steve Davies.....23
Giddy Up! Giddy Up!.....24
Shame on You.....26
Michelle Lilly.....28
Smells a Bit Fishy to Me.....29
Beth Finnerty Mitchell.....32
Tally Ho!....35
Sally Carter.....38
Trasi Lewis.....41
Clare Jones.....41
Ten Questions.....42

In The Name of God.....50
The Egg.....53
Steph Thomson.....55
Jonathan James.....58
What The Hell Are They Doing?.....61
You Don't Drink Milk?.....67
Angela R Stephens.....69
Mary Ann Coffey.....72
The Compassionate Mind.....73
You Are What You Eat.....75
The Great Spirit's Prayer.....78

Acknowledgements

I would like to give thanks to all those who participated in this project – Vegans and Non-Vegans. Thank you to my family for their love and support, thank you to all the folks who buy my books, and all my internet friends – who I frequently 'road test' my material on.

Introduction

This is my second Vegan work; 'The Vegan Vibrations' being the first. Both books concentrate on the *ethical* and *spiritual* aspect of Veganism – animals having consciousness is once again the topic. This time around however, things are a little 'different', the topics of fishing, horse-riding, dog fighting, hunting, and other acts of 'exploitation' are examined. In a 'controversial' decision, I have contributions from Vegans and non-Vegans! Really? Meat-eaters are having their say in this book? Yes, they certainly are!

I wanted this book to be 'bigger than life'! I wanted non-Vegans to 'have their say', without any 'backlash off myself or other Vegans – as it occurs frequently on the internet. I wanted the book to have a 'contrast' between opinions, a varied view of what Veganism means. So, buckle up, enjoy the ride, and of course – VEGAN POWER!

7

Questions from the foolish flock

Friday, 5th of June 2015:
It has been around about twenty three years since I 'discontinued' the eating of dead animals, and fast approaching my twenty third year as a Vegan. It has been a long ride; it seems like such a long time ago. At the time I was inspired by David Icke on the *BBC Radio 1* Nicky Campbell Show. David mentioned at the time that he was vegetarian, so I thought, 'why is he vegetarian?'... 'What is the specific reason for abstaining from animal flesh?'

During this period I was just starting my 'Spiritual Awakening': you know...when your head almost explodes! The feeling of isolation and loneliness, and the feeling of 'why am I behaving like this?'..'what is happening to me?' Obviously, the process of a 'Spiritual Awakening' involves energy changes: a shift in frequencies and a rising of mind and spirit. The connection between the conscious mind and subconscious mind becomes stronger...that is the rising force.

I was always the 'black sheep' or the 'lone wolf'; I tried to be sociable with whoever came my way, but I was obviously too 'different' to be accepted by my collective surroundings. Once I revealed I was vegetarian (Vegan shortly after) the questions came! At first, it was one big challenge! Once people find out any information on how or why you are behaving and thinking in an alternative universe to their own, they seemingly attack your views and comfort zone. 'Why is he like that?'...'He's trying to say that we are wrong in our eating patterns!'...'Who the hell is he to say that it is wrong to eat animals?'

With my studying of John Mellencamp, Bruce Springsteen, and David Icke interviews, I would remain pretty much calm when others would fire questions: I taught myself to listen, then answer. *The Godfather* movies were a big inspiration: how to stay calm in the storm, and 'reason' with those who are actually trying to bring you down.

After twenty three years of questions (mostly questions that are basically trying to 'catch you out') I am used to such nonsense! Every now and again, someone rears their ugly head with a stupid question, that has been repeated a million times before by other 'like minded' people. Sometimes, it is someone at work, in the pub, or maybe your partner will 'bring it up' to try and beat you! That last scenario: 'to beat you' is the 'king of annoyances' for Vegans. I often watch their beady little eyes; they are longing to put you in your place. They want to start the battle, humiliate you, and then brag about it to their fellow one dimensional (in terms of the 'attitude' towards animals) surroundings.

People do not want to question their own thought patterns or behavioural patterns; it is convenient to just 'fit in' and be one of the crowd. That way, they won't have to face the ridicule from being a little 'different', because the majority does not like 'different'...it goes against their pre-programmed mentality. Low and behold should you think for yourself! 'What would people think? What would the guys in work say if I revealed I was a vegetarian or having a spiritual awakening?' Oh my God! The shame of it all!

Let me tell you something: If I could care less about some one dimensional dimwit at work, or in the pub! When you begin to 'awaken', you will be challenged by those who refuse to go with the 'Truth Vibrations' or 'The Rising'... They are not your friends! They are 'irrelevant' people: if you let them, they will

break you. They haven't got the guts or strength to be their true'-selves, so in jealousy and frustration they attack. Do not misunderstand me here! I am talking about the minority of meat-eaters: most respect my views, and carry on without questioning me. The same goes with the topics of spirit, conspiracy, and general 'enlightened' thought patterns.
The questions! Oh how I love the questions and remarks by the 'prison farmyard' folk –
The list is probably endless, so I'll just list a few here:
'So, what do you eat then? Salads?'...
'That's why you are ill! It's because you don't eat meat!'...
'Well, animals have always been here for food!'...
'It's natural to eat meat, people have been eating it since time began'...
'It doesn't harm the cow when you milk it!'...
'It doesn't hurt the chicken by taking their eggs'...
'You Vegans are 'over the top'...
'You are not going to stop people eating meat or drinking milk, so what is the point? You are not making any difference!'....
....and so it goes with the unreasonable, one dimensional questions and remarks.

When closed minded people question me these days, I tend to stay calm for a while, then I get completely fed up with their low vibrational, energy wavelength. I raise my voice, and get slightly aggressive. Why? Well, after twenty three years of dealing with some stupid, jealous, bitter people – my patience has worn thin.

I always make it clear: I never preach about Veganism to people at work, in the pub, on the street, or to my partners and friends, because face to face, it's threatening to them. However, if I'm provoked by some mouthy 'know it all', I will go into Overdrive! I do not suffer fools! I preach on the internet, sure!

For example, the *Facebook* – it is *my* page, my book, my creation of words, pictures, and videos. If people do not like what I say or do on the internet, they can easily delete me, block me, or just simply ignore me.

Just one more thing (I'm sounding like *Columbo* now – Animals have consciousness: a soul. We are all part of the whole: God/ The Great Spirit. Love is everything: everything is energy vibrating at different speeds, the quicker the vibration – the more evolved the energy becomes (love is pure energy of the highest degree)..... Vegan Power!

I Don't Want to Die

Tally ho! Here they go...
Humiliation, Manipulation,
Getting ready at their battle stations:
In for the kill.
The passion, the glory, the smell of fresh blood...
The adrenalin pumps around their social circle...
Bonded by blood, by brotherhood, by stupidity.

Animals have souls?
They have a life force?
I don't believe such nonsense!
Tally ho! Here we go!
Another day in the killing fields;
Another breath of country air.
How dare they petition against our traditional lifestyle.

I am afraid, I am out of breath,
I am the hunted one.
What have I done to deserve this?
I have a family, I too have a social circle;
I have friends and loyalties.
I don't want to die;
I would like to enjoy and live out my natural life...
I pray...

Marcia Oldfield

At four years of age, I remember seeing my mum cutting up a pork chop on my plate, cutting it away from the bone, and I just knew then that it was wrong to eat a once living animal. I loved animals, and from that day refused to eat any meat, poultry, fish, eggs...all were animals in my mind.

Through school I was bullied for not eating meat even down to teachers trying to make me cut up bulls eyes in biology, and in my biology 'O' level I walked out of the classroom when the rat dissection started, and told the teacher I would be in the library – I just knew it was wrong. I have always felt that I have more compassion than my peers....I was considered freakish for my then vegetarianism, as I didn't then realise that dairy meant death too.

As soon as I educated myself (from getting leaflets from different societies, joining groups like Animal Aid, and even from a really informative health shop I used to visit in Chester that had posters of veal calves being slaughtered, and the abuse chickens suffered etc), I realised that the only way to totally avoid cruelty to animals was to become Vegan and not vegetarian.

If you talk to a lot of meat eaters, hardly anyone realises that male chicks get grinded up alive in the egg industry...that a lot of male calves are usually shot at a day old...this is all hidden and inconvenient to the meat and dairy industries...people want the comfort of blinkers on the reality of all the horror, so that they can partake in their snacks without any guilt ...I do not and never will.

I met my second husband and he was a full blown carnivore (even ate raw black pudding butties), and I knew if I shoved Veganism down his throat he would be kicking and fighting not to hear...so, slowly, slowly catchy monkey , I just educated him and he turned veggie, then vegan in about four years from meeting me....after he had found out that his meat diet had given him diabetes !!! Now, he will not touch meat, and that is through 'educating' not nagging him with the truth.

My three kids are all Vegan and are hardly ill, I think it's totally selfish to live your life eating tortured, murdered animals when you can live without it! I have been veggie / Vegan for 46 years, I cannot understand how someone can put flesh in their mouth, chew, and swallow it knowing that a few days before it was alive – too horrific.

I wish people had the compassion that I feel I have. I can survive without killing an animal, why can't they? If you cut me in half, I'd have Vegan written right through me...it is who/what I am foremost in my life...I have suffered for being one, but nothing could ever make me change.

14

Hell on Earth

Hell on Earth: testing on animals for cosmetics, drugs, the studying of human disease, and for medical training. A practice that is highly 'unacceptable' and 'unethical' to the degree of being totally absurd! In this day and age, it seems overwhelmingly unreal, but scientists and lab technicians still participate in the practice of animal testing.

It baffles me how some people actually agree on the principles of using animals as 'testing subjects', for in their eyes animals are secondary to humans – and therefore should serve humanity in any way possible. The cruelty and torture involved seems 'irrelevant' to these people; the manipulation of another species all adds up to a 'big so what'! How sad and pathetic has the human being become?

Cosmetic companies know very well that there are 'alternative' practises that can be used to test their products and ingredients – there is no need to torture, manipulate, kill, and induce suffering on our fellow creatures. Would you willingly test 'potentially harmful' substances and chemicals on your new born baby? Would you? How sick and twisted are you?

Innocent beings suffering at the hand of the greedy, selfish, 'uncaring' human – Has the world gone mad? Yes! The majority of the collective consciousness has become so 'one dimensional', so focused on the 'physical', that the real essence of life – the spirit, is ignored. The notion that animals have consciousness is laughed at by the majority (that is the picture I am viewing anyway!).

Apparently, around four million animals are experimented on

in British laboratories every year: rats, mice, cats, dogs, rabbits, guinea pigs, hamsters, fish and monkeys are used (or should I say 'abused'?) to test for anything from weed-killers, cleaning fluids, and food, to medical research into human disease, and also the development into producing new drugs. The pain, the misery, the frustration, and the heartache of being 'confined' into small cages, unable to express their 'natural instincts' and 'freedoms of movement' – is the 'soul destructive' manipulation by mankind.

Animals are cut open, blinded, electrocuted, or poisoned with various chemicals; most animals (if not all!) are 'terminated' after their experiment has come to an end. There is no compassion in these labs: they do the 'Devil's work' every day. How can they sleep at night, while abusing and murdering innocent beings day after day? – 'What goes around comes around' guys! What suffering you induce onto others will come back knocking at your door when you least expect it! It is called 'Karma' – a natural law of life.

Obviously, the 'awareness' of this particular problem has grown in strength by the growing number of people who are 'awakening', and are 'questioning' the behavioural patterns of the scientific establishment, and also the powers of the pharmaceutical company 'gangsters'! People are slowly recognizing the situation of animal abuse, whether it be animal testing, the diary industry, the meat industry, or any other 'abusive' behaviour towards the creatures of the Earth.

When humans are tortured, such as in times of war, aspects of terrorism, or maybe by sick and twisted serial killers – we regard these acts as barbaric and evil, but when the scenario becomes animal testing – it becomes 'acceptable' to the majority, and only the 'enlightened' minority kicks up a fuss.

I personally do not care what you believe! I care about what I believe! I will tell you directly and passionately – animals have consciousness, they have a soul. We are no better than our fellow creatures that roam this Earth; if anything they are better than us! It is the 'human' who causes pain and destruction on a global scale; it is the human who purposely manipulates the minds and bodies of the innocent and the seemingly weak.

There are alternative methods for the testing of cosmetics, food, and the research into diseases – without using and abusing the animal kingdom. In this day and age, technology is so advanced, there is no need to test on animals for any particular reason; mainstream science is 'dated', and relies on old traditional methods – it is 'static', it is cruel and unethical (especially on this particular topic!). Let modern science take over the roost: by 'modern science, I mean – a more 'open-minded' spiritual science that understands the 'natural laws' of energy, the realization that we are all one consciousness experiencing life as individuals and as a collective unit – while also using the advances of modern technology in a 'positive' fashion to create and maintain a well balanced environment for all beings to exist in harmony.

No animal testing, no abuse, no manipulation; no death – in the name of humanity's greed, no exploitation of freedoms, no disrespect of our fellow aspects of consciousness. Let there be love, let there be light, let there be equality between man and all creatures. In the name of Kingdom Come – let there be Peace.

Tracy Joy Aplin

I have always loved animals. My Mum said I should be a Vet, but the thought of animals dying was too much for me to bear. I never thought about what I ate, I just assumed we were meant to eat meat. My life literally changed overnight in 2007 when I got my first ferret; I was so in awe of such intelligence and personality in such a small animal – they form a real bond with you. When my ferret went missing after eighteen months, I realized how easily these creatures get lost, and how difficult it is to find homes for adult ferrets who sadly have a reputation for biting and smelling.

So I took in rescued ferrets. I had seven but am now back to three, losing most of them to old age. Lifespan is approx five to eight years. These little creatures really changed me; they became the entire focus of my life. Then I joined Facebook and started to learn the truth about the shocking animal industry. It was the video of the raccoon dog being skinned alive and thrown on top of a pile of carcasses, lifting its head to look at the camera, and blinking its long eyelashes that first opened my eyes.

In Feb 2001 I saw a request to do a 30 day Vegan Challenge for the month of March, and I breezed through it. My partner always cooked a Sunday pork roast; we use to fight over the crackling, and have friends or family over for dinner. He cooked one during my last week, and after our guests had gone home, and I was cleaning up, I pinched a tiny piece of meat. It tasted fatty, greasy, and completely unappetizing and foreign. I was glad I did that, and I think people should after 3 or 4 weeks because that's all it takes for your taste buds to change, and rather than craving food you use to enjoy, you realize that you don't actually enjoy it anymore and the cravings stop.

I am lucky that I never was a big cheese eater because I know it is almost addictive. So I haven't been the perfect Vegan since March 1st, 2001, but I know I will never go back to willfully eating animal products. The percentage of Vegans worldwide then was 1%, and I believe it is now around 3% with 10% vegetarian. I still have to research Vegan cleaning and beauty products. I knew if I tried to do everything at once I would most likely fail. I don't eat or wear animal products, except for a few knitted jumpers I inherited when my Mum passed away.

My partner is now Vegan at home. He is an interstate truck driver so finds it difficult on the road, but is now supportive of the Vegan philosophy. My only regret in life is that I had not become Vegan many years earlier, and raised my children Vegan with the hope that they would raise their children Vegan. I really think this is the way to move forward, through the children who have an inbuilt connection to animals.

I no longer take in rescued ferrets as they are obligate carnivores. I now take in orphaned herbivorous wildlife. I have two kangaroo joeys, three ring tailed possums, and a brush tailed possum. Every moment of my life revolves around animals, and I wouldn't wish for anything more, except to have my own kangaroo sanctuary. We live on half an acre which is enough room for about six roos, but hope to eventually move out of Suburbia and get ten or twenty acres. Vegan Power!

Your Children

The overwhelming frequency of being,
The undeniable truth before our eyes –
Ignored, washed away by the refusal to surrender.
Thou shall live in accordance to the energies of love, light, and righteousness.
All the creatures live in wonder, I often wonder...

Your children are lost, hurt, abused;
Your creations cry out in the wilderness.
What is the reason for so much suffering?
Is it Karma?
Is it something that we are unable to understand in this dense frequency?
I wish I knew the answer...

Give thy blessings to those in need,
Let the sky fall down, let the sky fall down...
The collective consciousness needs to be reborn, reinvented, revitalized.
Your children are in pain;
Only the minority cares.
The rising tide will wash away the sins of our conscious minds
– Hopefully.

I feel the pain,
I feel your frustration, your loss, your sadness.

Seek and you shall find?
We are looking for the answer –
We truly are.

Cats eyes, numbers and symbols, the Sun is my friend.
In the name of the Infinite Ghost –
I promise to find the pot of gold at the end of the rainbow,
I promise to remain focused in my passion for Truth, Love, and Compassionate behaviour.
And last but not least –
I will fight for the creatures of the Earth,
For they are my blood, my soul, my mind, my love.

Jahara Rhiannon

What Inspired Me to Go Vegan: I was involved with Animal Liberation activities in Melbourne: demonstrations against the fur trade, against the use of animals in circuses, vivisection etc etc, yet I wasn't even vegetarian. I was very shy, and didn't get to know other people who were also involved, so was not interacting and being influenced by anyone. But the hypocrisy was slowly infiltrating my brain.

The final catalyst for becoming Vegan happened when I went on a duck rescue. This involved wading through a lake during the Victorian duck shooting season, and rescuing injured birds and taking them back to the first aid tent. This was harrowing, upsetting beyond belief, and stressful.

At one point, a duck hunter was so angry at me 'stealing his' duck, that he aimed his gun at me and fired. In that second I knew I was going to die. A feeling of resignation came over me, that these were my last breaths. So when he missed, I was numb from shock. The guy was overtly drunk, and that, I presumed is what saved me. I remember hoping his aim was just as bad when he pointed his gun at the birds.

I went to the police who were there, to report this incident, but they were all out of uniform at that time in the day, and enjoying barbecued duck. They didn't care and didn't want to hear about it. It was after this weekend that the contradiction between working to save the lives of animals, standing up against the slavery, and my use of them, hit me hard. I stopped eating meat, and within about a month, I had become fully Vegan. At that time, over 25 years ago, I didn't know the word 'Vegan'. I only knew I didn't want to participate in the slavery in any way.

Aisha Sulayman

My husband says he eats meat because it's how he and most people were raised; he also said people are afraid of change, so they stay in there comfort zone. He said he don't mind vegan food sometimes, but don't think he could make the leap to live that lifestyle.

Nathan Budda Bowcott

Simply because I just love the taste of meat. Apart from meat, my diet is limited, as I am not a lover of most other foods. Plus it's the nicest, fastest way to get protein into your body.

Martyn Jones

I eat meat because I enjoy it, and I need to make no excuses for it. I would not become a Vegan for that reason alone. Also 'Andrew John Jones' asked for comments from meat-eaters for his book. Yet the very first one to comment is met with sarcasm and rude comments. I personally believe becoming a Vegan or not is a life choice, just like deciding whether to go to the pub on Friday night or not. Just because people eat meat does not make a Vegan a better person, so after the first comment made here, there should not even have been a response. The status says it all "meat-eaters only".

Martin Caviel

Turning Vegan is a big step, vegetarian is a step in the right direction, I no longer eat lamb for the reason you mention, and that has been for a number of years. It is a choice, I would find it hard to do, as I do not know enough about what foods to cook to replace the protein in meats, maybe one day!

Steve Davies

What has always got to me are the double standards of Vegans. They are quick to condemn meat-eaters, but will not bat an eyelid on the deforestation of rain forests, because of the growing demand for soya bean plantations. This destroys wild animals habitat which leads to their demise. I know you think meat eating is bad, but all humans, no matter what they eat are leading to the destruction of this beautiful planet. The mass production of selected fruit vegetables and other arable crops are doing more damage than we all would like to admit.

24

Giddy up! Giddy up!

The horse: what a beautiful creature. Now this may be controversial in the 'Vegan circles', but I personally do not believe in the riding of horses (or donkeys). 'Exploitation' is the word here – the using of another species, taking advantage of another being, the control of another life-form. I wouldn't fancy someone riding on my back! Whipping me, jerking and bouncing up and down! No thank you! Not today!

For me, it is unethical, it is far from being 'righteousness in motion'. A friend of mine once said that 'horse people' are not nice people (in terms of how they treat these beautiful creatures). She personally made the conscious decision to stop riding horses many years ago, and now runs and walks with her horses – giving the horses 'freedom' and the respect they truly deserve. She also said that the horse doesn't like the 'bit' in the mouth – come to think of it, neither would I!

Is horse riding 'Vegan'? I would say no. It is a form of manipulation; it is a form of control, control of another being. People who own horses might say (in defence of this particular topic) – 'horses need to be ridden for they need exercise ' – well, I am sure that a horse can run around by itself! I mean, the horse would enjoy the exercise without your 'weight' on it's back. Another 'defensive' comeback might be – 'the horse loves to be ridden!' – "Oh! So your horse talks to you? Or you have a 'mind to mind' connection with the horse? Clever ain't you? Very clever!"

As strong as they are, it can not be good for the horses frame, carrying the weight, the 'shocks' of the rider jerking up and down – surely! I am not saying you do not love or care for your horse or donkey; I am just 'examining' the aspects of this particular topic. Maybe Vegans are 'spilt' in their views on the subject matter of riding horses; maybe they are 'unsure' or 'undecided' of what is right and wrong.

My only 'experience' with horses wás with my friend (mentioned above); she truly loved and respected her fellow creatures. My thoughts at the time were how 'grand' these creatures were, obviously every creature has a 'personality', and horses are no exception. I remember us going up to the stables to see the horses, and clumsy 'ole' me getting stuck in the mud, while her horse stood on my foot – a painful little experience, let me tell you! I could see that they are very 'spiritual' creatures: you can see it in their eyes.

Whether it be horse racing, hunting, or general riding; whether you use whips, spurs, or gentle tapping – it is unethical in my view. Get off the horse! You are not in a Cowboys and Indians movie, it is 2015 folks! Walk! Catch a bus, a train, drive your car, or ride your bike. There is no excuse for using an animal for YOUR purpose.

Don't get me wrong, a lot of people who own horses keep them well fed, groom them well, and keep them in good living accommodations, but they seem to be ignoring the 'question' of is it 'ethical' or 'spiritual' to ride another aspect of consciousness? Maybe 'they know not what they do'? Maybe 'Vegan' horse-riders will be reading this piece, and are getting a bit 'disturbed' at the notion of 'it is wrong to take advantage of another species' – well, I am a writer, a thinker, a 'truth-seeker', it is my job to question everything!

So, 'Giddy up! Giddy up! – or not!

Shame on You

How long have you been Vegan?
What do you eat then?
So you just eat salads?
I couldn't live like that!
It is unnatural...
A good steak is what you want...

Bwark!
Bwark, bwark, bwark, bwark chicken!
Lay a little egg for me.
Eight egg omelettes? Really?
Is it also true that you would drink five pints of milk a day?

Greedy humans...
Unreasonable, uncaring humans.
Selfish beings of the earth:
Ignorant minds and heartless spirits.
Fools roam the Earth,
They know not what they do?
They know what they do...

Do not take your children to fast food junklets!
Educate yourself and your child...
How horrid is the notion of feeding your young a murdered being?
Blood fills the air;
All the folks in despair.
Who are you to judge our eating patterns?

27

Who are you to judge our behaviour in terms of animal usage?

I am a voice for the voiceless
In refusal to wear the shell of an innocent victim,
In refusal to drink the milk of another species,
In love with the notion of peace, love, and equality.
Leave them alone!
Leave them alone!

I was once a mind controlled slave;
I had no mind of my own.
Deep down in my heart and soul,
A burning flame of truth drip-fed my young mind.
One day, I rose from the ashes:
I knew I had it in me to be my true-self.

In the face of ridicule,
In the light of my past experience –
I stood tall.
I blew away the doubters, the clowns, the fools, and the sleeping puppets of the farmyard mentality.
You participate in the killing, in the abuse, in the manipulation of The Great Spirit's children.
Shame on you!
Shame on you!

Michelle Lilly

My thoughts on animal rescue: I think this is the stickiest part of Veganism. I have personally helped hundreds of dogs be rescued and adopted. I have 11 personal dogs of my own at home. One day I realized that the more dogs I rescue, the more other animals are dying to feed them, and it isn't animal for animal. For every one dog, how many animals must die? A thousand chickens? A hundred lambs? Twenty cows? What about for every hundred dogs? One hundred thousand chickens – ten thousand lambs – two thousand cows? And, so on.

It grows exponentially. In saving dogs and cats, we are directly contributing to killing "other" animals for dog/cat food. Talk about speciesism! It is a disproportionate number of animals that must be killed to feed a single "pet" like a dog or cat. One option is to feed dogs a Vegan diet, which is not difficult to do. Easy peasy, but controversial. Cats can be done, but it is more difficult and more controversial. I can control this in my home by feeding my dogs what I consider to be an ethical and healthful diet based on my years of research, but if I am helping dogs be saved and get adopted out to other families, I cannot control what they eat; so I am, therefore, contributing to the death of other animals.

It is a massive conundrum. I do not know what the answer is. I stress about this all the time. We can't euthanize all the dogs and cats, obviously, that is a terrible answer – But, some thought needs to go into this! It is just another reason to control pet overpopulation and get people to stop mindlessly and thoughtlessly getting pets as trinkets or "amusement" that they have no business getting.

29

Smells a bit fishy to me!

The fisherman: he or she couldn't care less about the 'beings' that are being murdered every single day. To the fisherman (I will stick to the term 'fisherman', for a 'wo-man' is 'man' – our souls/spirits are Male and Female energy, so go and figure!) – fish are seemingly 'irrelevant'. Because fish do not 'cry out' in pain, apparently, they feel no pain! Well, that is the 'defensive', ignorant response you will probably get from those who fish.

'Oh! I throw the fish back in the water! It's okay – they don't feel a thing!' Well, bless my cotton socks and gloves! You fishing folks must be right! I mean, you believe it so passionately, you really got me here! Mmmmm? Okay!

Let me sit you down in my classroom; I will teach you about Energy, Life, Death, Love, and The Great Spirit. Not interested? Okay! Keep your head in the sand then.....

Fish are aspects of Infinite Consciousness, they have a 'soul', or a 'spirit'; they are 'part of the whole' – they exist in this dream-scape reality just as we do. We live on land; fish live under water (obviously!). They actually communicate and interact with each other through low frequency sounds; they are capable of learning and socializing within their selected groups.

Fish feel pain! I said fish feel pain! Would it hurt you if I put a hook through your mouth, and then pulled it back out again? Would you feel the pain if I slit your belly with a sharp knife, and let you slowly bleed to death? You have seen a fish shaking and struggling on the end of a line; wriggling on a fishing boat deck, with the many other 'aspects of consciousness' – in pain, in fear, in the stressful experience of potential death.

Sitting by the riverside, 'c'mon fishies, c'mon!' – how nice! How relaxing! How pathetic, when you realize the 'Truth'! The only difference between a human, a dog, and a fish, is the physical 'shell' the soul resides in. We are all children of The Great Spirit – or 'The Infinite One'. It does not matter the size of the being, the shape of the being, or the colour of the being, we are all one 'Love'.

Some folks may laugh at the notion of fish having consciousness – 'fish have a soul? Hahaha! Don't be so silly! They are just fish!' Ignorance has blinded the already 'blind'. I remember many years ago, I would cycle up into the countryside and pass the fishermen along the banks of the reservoir. I would say to myself, 'I hope you catch nothing! I hope you fail all day in your attempts to abuse the fish!' I have no time for those who manipulate and abuse animals; the information and knowledge is abundant in today's times for what is righteous and what is downright WRONG!

Studies have shown that fish have senses, and react to pain; if you are travelling in a 'physical' body – you obviously have senses and energy 'reactions' to various experiences. Whether it be angling, netting, hand gathering, or spearing, fishing is 'unethical' – just as killing a dog, a cat, or a cow is unethical.

Teaching your children to fish or hunt – well, that is downright absurd! In this day and age, most people refuse to go with the rising vibrations of righteousness and truth; most people seemingly are so comfortable in their 'own little world', that the ideals of what is right and what is wrong are almost irrelevant, almost non-existent!

We live in a cruel world: animals and people are abused, manipulated, and mistreated to the highest of extremes. Does anyone care? The 'minority' cares! There is a growing, rising energy force that will eventually 'win through' – I honestly can not see it 'changing fold' a hundred percent in my lifetime, but, I think as the years roll by, there is a significant difference to the collective consciousness, in terms of 'respect' for one another, and respect for our fellow creatures of the land and sea.

How can you not see the 'truth' in the centre of the circle? It is there I tell you! Can you not see or 'feel' the connection, when you see the eyes of another species? – if 'something' moves from A to Z, and maybe has eyes, it has a 'soul' – well, more than likely!. We do not need fish, or any other 'murdered' being for food and nourishment: we are capable of living off the land. People need to 'question' their thoughts and behavioural patterns, for their 'selfishness' is creating a 'disturbance' in the force.

Beth Finnerty Mitchell

Why did I turn vegan?
As a small child, I was regularly fed meat. From memory, our Sunday dinners always consisted of roast beef and Yorkshire pudding. My parents were Welsh and English and considered that meat made for a good and strong constitution. I was always encouraged to eat it.

When I was younger, about six years of age, I always asked questions about everything (nothing much has changed), but then I recall one Sunday, in particular. I said to my mum, 'where did this meat come from?' and mum replied with, 'it's from the butcher'. I further questioned what a butcher was, and mum stated it was where you bought meat. 'Where does meat come from', I asked? Mum then said an animal. I asked what type of animal, and to my absolute horror, mum said a cow. My dad then replied with "poor bastard", he didn't like to eat meat and seldom did. My father use to have a sticker on his car – which read "be kind to animals", and I will never forget that Sunday as it will be etched in my mind forever.

Years went by and I never liked meat, in fact I really hated it, but still ate it, and never enjoyed it. I thought it was doing me good. I never really thought outside the box, and I still drank and ate dairy, even though I disliked it. What an absolute fool I was – I know now, but I was still pondering, then.
It wasn't until I turned 40 that I became a vegetarian: I realised that whatever I was eating was making me sick, and caused weight gain. I dropped the meat, but I still drank milk and ate dairy.

I worked in a government agency, whereby morning teas were plentiful, and so were cheese and crackers and cream cakes. When I look back, I was evolved enough to realise. Even though I was a highly educated being – I was so dumb.

As a result of all this, I wasn't feeling good – I always felt full, and sick in the stomach, even consuming a skinny cafe latte, made me feel ill-ish. So In 2012, and after many years of enduring an upset stomach, feeling sluggish, throat infections, heartburn, SOL (shit on liver), and feeling under the weather, I decided enough was enough and it was time to go Vegan. My sister's family were Vegans, so I thought if they could do it, so could I and I did! My young nieces taught me how, and showed me what was what in the supermarket. Evolved kids!! Thanks, to Courtney, Holly and Maddy!

In the three years I have been Vegan, I have lost fourteen kilos in weight, I never get sick, never feel nauseas; have not had any reflux or colds, I now have a good and healthy disposition in life. I am also more mentally aware. People say, I look younger (which is always a good thing)!

I abhor cattle trucks, and always give the driver the "bird", as I overtake him. He has no clue why I birdied him, but I do! I loathe animal cruelty and feed the wild birds daily; I also have seven stray cats that I feed, twice daily (crazy cat lady, they call me). I do my best to educate the wider community about becoming a Vegan and give regular donations to animal charities.

Unfortunately, where my business is located, the smell of fresh fish, roasting chicken, pork, beef or lamb, fills the air and mostly makes me violently ill. Nothing is Vegan not even the Sushi (as it has mayo), which is made with egg. So I bring my own lunches to work, as we Vegans get so hungry, but not hungry enough to eat a horse! Pardon the pun!

I wear and only purchase Vegan make –up, which is difficult for me as I am a beautician and own my own franchise. I don't buy or wear leather anything – or fur, and have given my woolly jumpers away. I mistakenly drank honey by accident the other day – and was nearly sick!

I feel I am a better human being now, and I feel so very proud of whom I have become. I was just trying to evolve into a better person, and even though it took many years, I finally have mastered the art, and truly, once and for all conquered it. Go me!

Tally-ho!
(The hunt)

Tally-ho! A phrase largely used by British hunters with bloodthirsty hounds; a 'shout' that is to encourage the dogs to seek out the 'victim' of the hunt (whether it be a fox or any other innocent animal). Shame on you! Shame on you! That is what I say....

This is 2015 – a time when we should be civilised in our behaviour towards our fellow creatures. Why do people hunt? Well, some do it for the 'thrill', the 'social bonding' between certain groups of people (somewhat like a special club – if you like...), while others do it as a 'competitive sport'. Yes folks, in this day and age, people still hunt poor defenceless creatures – sad, but true!

These are the same one dimensional people who probably believe that animals have no consciousness; animals are 'just there'! That is their low level of thought. There is no glory in murder! It is a low vibrational energy pattern; it is a cowardly act of selfishness and thoughtlessness.

Hunting for food: there are plenty of food resources in the plant kingdom – we do not need to kill animals for their flesh. This is not 'the age of the caveman' – all the nutrition we need to live and survive can be found in 'plant food' (Veganism).

Hunting as a sport: 'really? I mean really?' Murder as a sport! Yes, I know people have killed animals in a 'sporting fashion' for hundreds of years, but it is downright wrong and unethical!

Hunting as a 'traditional' social gathering (such as fox hunting): chasing a fox for hours, stressing the fox to the maximum of its physical, mental, and spiritual limits – how lovely of you guys to do that! Then as the fox is grounded, it is dug out and ripped apart by the hounds (or sometimes just shot). What a beautiful gathering that must be. Tell me, 'is the being we call Satan present in these hunts? – or maybe satanic energy resides in your twisted minds?'

'Well, animals kill and hunt other species for food, they do it to live and survive – it is in their natural instincts!' Yes, I know! I am not stupid! I also know that originally, humans and animals didn't need physical food for energy: obviously, I am going back thousands and thousands of years ago. They lived and survived just like they do in the afterlife, or the 'spirit worlds' – their energy came from 'Faith'. This Faith or 'belief' is simply an understanding of energy: we exist because we believe we exist. Our soul or spirit does not need beans and chips or bananas and carrots to survive: it is pure love, pure consciousness, pure 'energy'.

Somewhere along the line, the collective consciousness got 'poisoned' by a highly negative source; the frequencies of life on Earth became more and more dense. Everything is energy vibrating at different speeds: the quicker the vibration – the higher the frequency. Therefore, a slow vibration is one of ignorance, darkness, selfishness, and a refusal to spiritually 'evolve'. Whereas the 'quicker' vibration is one of understanding, compassion, love, and a 'determination' to spiritually evolve.

So, I am saying that originally animals and humans did not need 'physical' food, they didn't need to hunt; they just 'existed'. I wonder if that story of *Adam and Eve* is 'symbolic' of the 'poisoned' collective consciousness? Maybe! I mean, as soon as *Eve* took the apple from the tree, and took a bite, all hell broke loose! It is only a story, I know, but there are a lot of 'symbolic' stories in books of religion that have a 'hidden' meaning.

Hunting is violence – simple as! Many animals endure long, slow deaths during a hunt or a 'chase', and there is no justification for the process. Cruelty is 'negativity': the opposite end of the spectrum to compassion and understanding. Whether you go rabbiting with your spaniels, elephant shooting, bird shooting, trapping – you are a murderer!

Obviously, in some parts of the world, and in 'so called' controlled conditions, hunting is allowed in some fashion – and these people sleep at night! Shocking I know! Animals have 'family units', just as we humans do. They make friends, they bond, they love – and these guys shoot them! Breaking up and disturbing the 'family' environment, stressing the other members of the group or pack. There is no excuse for killing an aspect of consciousness – or for simply creating 'fear' during a 'chase'.

What do people hunt? Well, you know the mentality of the 'hunter': backward, twisted, and evil – anything from foxes, rabbits, and deer, to bears, elephants, and birds. Nothing is too big for the hunter! The bigger the better, I guess. They have no compassion, no love, no understanding of the natural laws of the universe.

The hunting 'mentality' also fights for the notion of – hunting is an essential part of 'pest control' in the countryside or in natures 'back garden' so to speak. 'Oh right! So you chase and torture them in the name of population control or pest control?' It has nothing to do with the 'thrill' of the hunt of course – yeah right! What is the difference from working in a slaughterhouse, killing cows, sheep, and pigs all day, to hunting rabbits or foxes? There is no difference! A kill is a kill! There is no 'righteousness' in murder: to take a life is to create a disturbance in the forcefield of the collective consciousness. May God have mercy on your sorry souls; the animals may forgive you – but I do not!

Sally Carter

My Journey to Veganism:
I was born and brought up in the 'Chiltern Hills' in Buckinghamshire. I am a practising SGI Nichiren Buddhist, and now also a Vegan! Divorced, I have two grown up sons of twenty nine and twenty seven. I work for the NHS, and have two wonderful dogs, which I adore.

As a child I spent most summers up the fields, building camps in the bales, walking fields with cows in, accidently treading in cow pats, and visiting farms; I'd look lovingly into their eyes, while stroking them, not knowing their fate. Never noticing when they had gone from the field, and the next herd had arrived, I never questioned it. This was childhood innocence and ignorance, and then grew up with adult ignorance.

Leaving school at sixteen, I went to work on a farm which was primarily arable, with just a hand full of sheep – which I rarely had an involvement with. On a couple of occasions my mate and I helped to move them from one field to the next. By this time my sister worked for a large supermarket chain, and was transferred to the meat room, where her experience didn't last long, and she became a vegetarian. Her experience had no impact on me. We all live different lives and have different experiences.

I have never been a huge meat eater, but the decline in my consumption of meat happened after the 'Mad Cow' saga. It was nearly two years ago, about August 2013, that I was viewing my posts on Facebook. My eyes caught a post, a clip from the film '*Samsara*', the six minute 'food section' – what I saw shocked me to the point that I thought this is not real, this is not right, is it?? It showed a large wheel going around in a circle, with fifty or more cows on it being milked, not the usual conventional farm milking. It also showed a chicken processing plant in China or Thailand, where the workers were dressed in disposable all in one overall and face masks, obviously for food hygiene, but they looked like they should have been working in a nuclear reactor plant. Beside them, there were conveyor belts and hundreds of chicken strung up being processed. Big, Huge shock!!

I decided to investigate further, watching PETA's *'If slaughterhouses had glass walls'*. I had never thought or consider what a slaughterhouse was before, but what I saw touched the deepest part of being. The sadness that welled up inside of me was indescribable, and I sat in tears at my computer. That was my turning point; I'd had the 'light Bulb' moment. Veganism has been a gradual process, and will be on going as we don't live in a Vegan world. So it will be continually checking ingredients in foods.

In the beginning, it was a struggle to give up eggs, though I only ate them now and again. If I go out, as most restaurants do not serve Vegan food, and they think vegetarians live on cheese, I have found a lovely little cafe selling vegetarian/Vegan food locally. Veganism is a journey of discovery, compassion for living beings, making the best choices of healthy delicious food, and becoming more adventurous in the kitchen – baking vegan cakes, which no one can tell the difference.

The bigger picture of Veganism is not just about food, it's toiletries, shoes, tyres, handbags, belts, furniture, dog food, sweets, just to mention a few... arh good old Haribo which I had an addiction too, until I discovered what gelatine was made of! The list of products goes on and on.

Most people say they love animals, but see farm animals differently, and call them 'Livestock' and 'Beef', they are cows. People get up in arms when they here of Chinese eating dog...What is the difference? There is not any difference, they are living breathing animals that deserve our compassion and respect. Cows can live up to the age of twenty five years old, so slaughtering at fourteen months when they are babies, and slaughtering calves at four months for veal is wrong in so many ways.

I know I have made the right choice to be Vegan, morally, and I can live with myself and sleep at night. Though several people do not like my ideas, they choose to bury their heads in the sand. To not eat meat is a compassionate thing to do and a healthier life to be lived. It doesn't matter how long the journey to Veganism takes, every step counts for less suffering of animals. I also feel strongly about animal testing.

We live in the Twenty first century, put man on the moon, and invented the most destructive thing known to man – 'the atom bomb', but still live in a primitive world of animal testing. Humanity has to wake up and see the cruelty. Through social media, people are able to access information. Though the process is slow, I believe things are changing!

Trasi Lewis

I am a failed Vegan: I was Vegan for about eighteen months, but have been a Veggie for thirty odd years. I cannot understand why people want to eat flesh of an animal. I turned Vegan after having information through the post! – it was *Viva*. I have never worn leather, because I don't eat it, won't wear it, same as anything tested on animals. What is the point of not eating animals, or their by products, when some people I knew at the time spent money on food made by large companies that use animal testing! I have two children: a fourteen year old boy, and a nine year old girl – both have been brought up 'veggy' and are proud to be...

Clare Jones

Vegan – for the animals, the horror they go through, the injustice of the lives that don't have a chance. To help the planet. Whatever normal is, Vegan is normal for me, as I gave up meat aged eleven, and dairy in 1993.

Ten Questions
(Steph Thompson and Andrew J Jones)

Here we have My friend Steph Thompson, who willingly gave me ten questions on Veganism. Steph is not Vegan: I wanted a 'meat-eater' to ask me questions (I wanted there to be a 'contrast' in this book, a wide opinion on the topic of Vegansm. Thank you Steph....

Steph Thompson: I think that this is an important exchange, because too often I see people with different ideas about diet and lifestyle choice, such as ourselves, who are aggressive and intimidating towards one another. Nobody should be made to feel bad about the choices they make for themselves, but there is nothing wrong with debate, persuasion, and challenges of ideology.

1 – You have said that you used to be vegetarian for a while. Why did you go that one step further and become Vegan?

I became Vegetarian in December 1992, after being 'inspired' by a radio interview between Nicky Campbell and David Icke. David said in the interview that he was a Vegetarian, so I thought, 'why is he vegetarian?' – 'What is the idea behind that?' So I questioned myself and my thought patterns, and carried out the 'vegetarian lifestyle'. A few months later, I was getting really frustrated at my acne problems: my face and chest in particular – so I thought, 'if I cut out the milk and eggs in my diet, would my skin improve?' Well, after so many weeks, my skin did not improve – but! And a big 'but'! I once again examined and 'questioned' the idea of being a Vegan, and decided that it is 'ethically' and 'spiritually' the right thing to do. Almost twenty three years later – here I am! Vegan Power!

The realization that all beings have consciousness 'hit me like a hammer'; this was an important change for me at the time. A period of an 'awakening' began: the enlightenment came from within and without – books, radio interviews, films, music, and my own 'writings'. My inspired mind took me to the path of righteousness. This period was actually the beginning of 'self-awareness', I guess. Although I am Vegan, that is only one 'aspect' of who I am. I am a 'multi dimensional' being – there are many aspects or pieces to a soul/mind spirit.

2 – I have heard that there are different levels of Veganism. Is this true and would you explain what the differences are for us?

Firstly, I will explain the difference between a vegetarian and a Vegan: a vegetarian is one who does not eat the flesh of an animal (meat), but does 'consume' dairy, eggs, and (some) eat fish. A Vegan is one who abstains from all animal produce: no meat, no eggs, no dairy, no leather, no honey, no fish – anything that 'derives' from another species is simply 'unacceptable'.

Of course, you also have the 'inbetweeners' – the part time veggies, who nine times out of ten, simply cut out meat, eggs, or diary for their health (and not for the ethical reason of 'compassion'). They are 'termed' by multiple names: lacto-vegetarians – meat and eggs are 'allowed', but they do not consume diary. Lacto-ovo vegetarians – avoid all meat, but consume eggs and diary. Pescatarians – avoid poultry and meat, but consume fish (some believe it 'acceptable' to eat eggs and diary – a personal choice?). In terms of Veganism, there is Veganism, and raw Veganism – which is basically nuts, seeds, fruit, and vegetables (a diet consisting of unprocessed raw vegan foods, that have not been heated above 115 degrees fahrenheit – that is what the 'raw foodists' adhere to – apparently, anything above 115 degrees 'ruins' the nutritional value of the food). There is also the Fruitarian diet or 'lifestyle' – which is in most part fruit based (although some nuts, seeds, and vegetables can be added to the diet – again, depending on personal choice, and what the 'term' Fruitarian means to the individual)

As for 'levels' – who made that stuff up? Levels? The above is self explanatory! 1 to 4? 1 to 5? I really don't take much notice of such 'irrelevant' information.

3 – Dolphins have been classed as non-human persons due to their intelligence, communication, and self-awareness. However, they also harm and sexually abuse their own kind. As a similarly flawed species, why should we not also eat fish?

Yes, it is true that dolphins are highly intelligent creatures; however, I had to google the 'sexually abuse' part. I have just found an article on this particular topic, stating that males have been known to 'forcefully' mount other males, to show their 'authority'. Apparently, it is a 'show of strength'! – to dominate other males from other groups. Well, you learn something new every day! Flawed species? I think most beings, whether human or animal are flawed.

The collective consciousness has been 'poisoned' by highly negative energies: in effect, that has 'blurred' the connection between our conscious minds (the lower level of oneself) and our subconscious minds (the higher level) – therefore, the world we live in appears to be a much darker place than originally intended. Once you lose the connection, all hell breaks loose! I honestly believe that 'in the beginning' humans and animals survived without consuming 'physical' food; they lived as they do in the spirit worlds – just existing! Then as time went by, you could say 'something happened on the way to heaven' – as I have said, the collective consciousness somehow got 'poisoned' by a highly negative force, and this physical world became more 'dense'. The vibrational energy of the planet and it's people was 'slowed down'; therefore, the frequency became (as I have said) dense.

Why should we not eat fish? I believe that fish have 'consciousness', they have a soul – they feel love, they feel pain, they make friends, and they are 'social' beings.

4 – How do you respond to the idea of third world countries using milk and cheese to sustain malnourished members of their population in the event of a crop failure?

Good solid question! Ethically, it is still 'using' animals: using the animals to feed the humans. If you do not take the 'dairy', the humans will die? Children will die? The problem in the world (in terms of the poor 'third world' countries) is the fact that there is a 'surplus' of food at all times. There are plenty of resources on this planet to feed every one of us ten times over!

The question: 'then how are so many starving and dying in third world countries?' – The big problem is that so much land in the world is used to grow 'feed grain' for the animals; obviously those 'fattened' animals are used for meat and dairy. The consumption of animal produce actually causes 'human hunger' – when viewed from this perspective.

There is plenty of food and grain for the world to live

'comfortably', but the 'greed' from the meat and dairy industry steals the lives away from these 'under developed' countries. Do you actually think that these 'big shots' in their business suits care about the thousands or maybe millions of starving people in poor countries? They do not! They are ruthless, uncaring, evil almost!

But with that question still 'unanswered' – do you feed the animal produce to the starving if their crops have been unsuccessful? The solution lies within the context of the problem: if 'Veganism' became the 'majority' there would be less hunger in the world. The notion of feeding animal produce to the poor folks that have had an 'unsuccessful' crop sickens me a little, because sentient beings are being 'manipulated' into play, they are 'abused' to supply the needs of the human. It is a 'tricky' question, but an important one!

5 – Leading on from my previous question, if it meant literal life or death to a human, are milk, eggs or meat OK if they are the only way to keep someone alive?

Okay, there are always 'scenarios' about – 'if you were on an island, and there was no food except a cow (or any other animal), would you eat it?' If it was the only way to keep someone alive? There is no clear 'scenario' here, so, I would say to choose human over animal is 'ethically' and 'spiritually' wrong! All beings are equal: it was 'Man' who decided that we should 'rule over beast'.

A 'scenario' would be: if your child was starving on an island, there was no food, but there was an animal – would you kill it to keep your child alive? My answer to that particular question would be? I really don't know! If I kill the animal, I am a murderer; if I let my child die for the lack of food – It is a hard question! Probably the hardest of the bunch! I like to think that I am not 'enlightened' enough to answer the question, but either way, or on 'both sides of the coin' it is an 'epic fail' in terms of compassion and living the 'spiritual' life. Good question though!

6 – Rightly or wrongly, our ancestors ate meat to help them survive. Is it part of a universal plan that they did that, and if so, was meat eating always wrong?

As I have already explained, the collective consciousness became 'poisoned', and the 'human' began to slow down the vibrational energy of life, so everything became 'dense', everything became more 'physical' than 'spiritual'.

What probably happened 'way back when', is that the slowing down of the Earth's frequencies, the 'individual', and the collective consciousness affected the existence of every living thing, and I can only guess, but, I think that originally, due to the 'slowing down', the human and the animal started to eat from the trees and the ground.

As time went by, and obviously our 'energy of life' was vibrating at even slower speeds, beings started to hunt and kill for food. The slower the vibrational turn – the more 'negative' the outcome.

7 – As a meat eater I have heard and seen comments and memes designed explicitly to disgust, shame and shock me about my diet choice, which have been created and shared online by Vegans. Should Vegans refrain from this sort of extremism or does the end justify the means? This is, ultimately, causing distress to an animal, namely, me.

With their 'passion' for animal rights, Vegans can be extreme at times, myself included! I think a lot of Vegans on the *Facebook* for example, are 'VEGAN! VEGAN! VEGAN!' – it 'drives' their lives in a way. There is nothing wrong with that of course, it is all for a good cause. The aggressive behaviour towards meat-eaters? Well, I guess – when provoked, Vegans will 'defend' their beliefs. At the end of the day, Vegans are 'the voice for the voiceless'.

I do understand your view and concern though; some Vegans may go 'over the top' – but a lot of meat-eaters do the same thing. 'Aggressive' behavioural patterns are not the way forward – obviously! I sometimes 'loose my rag' with questioning meat-eaters, for nine times out of ten, it is not through interest – but more to 'catch me out'! How do I know that? Through twenty three years of Vegan experience.

8 – Should a Vegan parent offer meat choices to their children, and if not, how would they defend taking away the child's right to choose?

Personally, I have no children, but I will 'speak my mind' anyway: a 'true' Vegan parent would not offer animal produce to their young. To me, it is no different to giving them beer or drugs! 'Unethical' in the highest possible sense! When the child is old enough he/she can 'choose' and do whatever the hell they want I suppose, but if I had a child, and my partner was Vegan too, the child would be brought up on a plant based diet.

Is it 'controlling' to dictate to your own children of what they are having on their plate? In this particular scenario – no! What is on the plate is ethically and morally acceptable to the ideals of 'respect' for all living things.

9 – Do Vegans agree with the use of woollen clothing?

Most do not wear wool: wool, obviously comes from an animal, so therefore it is 'derived' from another being. The wool industry is basically an 'exploitation' of another species. Farmers do not shave the sheep out of 'compassion' or love – they do it as a business. The wool industry is a huge money making business, and as with the dairy industry, when the animal is less 'productive' as age comes on us all – the animal is then taken to slaughter. It is ONE – TWO – THREE: breed, use, kill. Using an animal is a 'manipulation' of ones rights as an aspect of consciousness.

10 – As you may well know, egg tempera was used to make paint since Egyptian times. Many of the great 'masterpiece' paintings that have inspired the world and lifted poor and ordinary people out of the difficulties of their lives have used this medium. Would you destroy those paintings, knowing how they were made?

Being a bit of an artist myself, I would not 'destroy' great works of art, for in this day and age, we have access to so much knowledge – the internet being 'king' of course. We have access to the relevant information about 'animal rights' and 'Veganism', so there is no excuse for ignorance (when it comes to the respect of all animals). Maybe some of the artists of yesteryear were 'blind' to the total compassion of animals – maybe they just didn't realise about the 'ethics' of using animal produce.

  The world is starting to vibrate at a higher speed; you wouldn't think it, watching the television, or reading the newspapers of course, but more and more people are 'awakening'.

In the name of God

Religion: Oh, how I love stories 'apparently' written by God! The best writer ever! Well, that is not exactly true – I believe that books of religion were written by people 'high up' in secret societies 'many moons' ago (that is what I believe: you can believe whatever you want!)

Killings and sacrifices in the name of God! How pathetic! Do you actually think the being known as God, The Great Spirit, Allah, Infinite Consciousness – wants us to kill and sacrifice animals? The 'all knowing', loving, peaceful creator of all that has been, all that is, and all that will be – appreciates murder? How utterly ridiculous and absurd to even think that!

LEAVE THE ANIMALS ALONE! They are 'part of the whole'; they are aspects of consciousness. Man: the destructive being, that not only manipulates the creatures of the Earth, but the Earth itself in every way possible – a 'wrecking ball'!

Many animals are 'ritually' slaughtered while still conscious: apparently, some 'religious notion' of there must be as much blood as possible, for the 'life-force' of the animal is in the blood – and therefore that is the 'offering' to the God. Religion portrays itself as 'spiritual', yet, it participates in murder! In some religious festivals or 'events', thousands of animals are slaughtered under the name of the 'religion of the day'! What the hell is going on? – And we stand for this 'barbaric' nonsense!

A lot is based on 'fear': people of various faiths are afraid to question the words and meanings of their religious books – for they will be shunned, ridiculed, and in some 'strict' religions killed! I made the choice many years ago to be 'a religion of one' – I question everything, I think for myself, I have a mind of my own! It must be really 'difficult' being born into a 'strict' religion'; as I have said, once you question the principles of the 'book', you are automatically 'hated' by your fellow man (I use the term 'man', for it is in the context of hu-man – so, obviously, the wo-man applies too).

Let me give you a couple of examples from around the world on animal 'ritual' sacrifice:

Eid al-Adha (Festival of Sacrifice) – A Muslim celebration of 'remembrance', when Allah appeared to Ibrahim in a dream, asking for a 'sacrifice' of his son Ishmael – a showing of his 'loyalty' and love for the 'Almighty One'. Apparently, the Devil intervened, and told Ibrahim to 'spare' Ishmael, but Ibrahim was just about to go through with the sacrifice, and Allah stopped him – and gave him a ram to sacrifice instead. So he seemingly passed the 'test' of his loyalty to the 'Almighty One'. A similar story is also told in the Christian *Old Testament*, when God asks Abraham to sacrifice his son Isaac.

So today, in 'symbolic' fashion of your 'loyalty' to Allah, an animal is killed (sacrificed). Well, actually, millions of animals are killed/sacrificed around the world on this three day festival.

The Gadhimai Hindu festival (Nepal): An event that involves a 'huge' sacrificial slaughter of animals – water buffaloes, goats, pigs, chickens, pigeons, and rats. Apparently, this festival is to 'praise and please' Gadhimai – the goddess of power.

Can you imagine the cries and sounds of pain and misery? The smell of fresh blood in the air; the fear and confusion of all those 'thousands' of animals murdered in the name of a 'goddess'! In 2009, 200,000 animals and birds were sacrificed at the Gadhimai Hindu festival – that is absolutely disgusting!

God is loving, compassionate, and understanding; God is Male and Female energy. Let me tell you something: God, The Great Spirit, Allah, Infinite Consciousness (all multiple names for the 'Almighty One') is not happy with the behavioural patterns of Man against Animal. Would God kill one of its own children? Every man, woman, and animal is an aspect of The Great Spirit or God – Murder is unacceptable!

I am a 'Religion of One'; I do not believe in your 'version of events'. I do not believe in the 'black and white' of your books – most of which are symbolic, and are not to be taken literally by the 'wise', and the 'truth-seeking' beings who desire 'Spiritual Evolution'. Shame on you! For the murders of our fellow creatures in their 'hundreds and thousands' as the years roll by – in the name of Religion! I shake my head in disgust!

May God have mercy on your souls....

The Egg
(Reprinted from 'The Vegan Vibrations')

What came first? The chicken or the egg? – Never-mind that nonsense! The 'Egg' – in essence, the start of a 'physical' life (and if fertilized, potentiality in motion). Why would you possibly want to consume another species 'waste-product'? 'Why 'O' why?' It derives from 'tradition' of course: your parents may have eaten eggs, your grandparents, and so it goes....

To me, personally, I believe it is so 'disrespectful' to the other species – to take their eggs and 'eat them'! It is quite a 'horror' in fact! Personally, it is no different to sucking your dogs tits for milk! The scenario is no different in my eyes; ridiculous in every 'spiritual' and 'ethical' wave that I ride on.

Male chicks are separated from their sisters at birth, and are 'destroyed' – by 'grinding' or by being thrown into giant 'trash-cans' to suffocate and starve. The reason: male chicks are of 'no use' to the 'egg industry', they are deprived of a 'natural' physical life or existence.

Apparently, domestic hens 'bred' by humans, are able to lay around 300 (unfertilized) eggs per year – obviously, a strain on the hens physical system! But, does 'Farmer brown' care? He does not! Chickens are a 'money-making' device to the farmer; to an 'ethical' Vegan however, they are aspects of Infinite Consciousness.

Male chicks are killed by the 'hundreds of thousands' every day! Every time you buy a carton of eggs, you are contributing your 'energy' to the murder of 'millions' of male chicks – not nice, hey? A hens 'natural' life is apparently between 15 and 20 years – but, because of the 'horrid' conditions that they are kept in (they are regarded as egg and meat machines!), their lifespan is cut short to probably around the two year mark.

'Surely, it is okay to eat 'unfertilized' eggs?' – 'You are not killing anyone?' Well, aside from the above information, why would you want to eat the 'waste' product of another species? It has no logical or spiritual 'standing'.

I stand by my thought patterns here: An Egg is the start of a physical life (obviously, when fertilized it becomes a life!) – but, just the 'idea' of the notion that it is 'potentially' a new life, makes it a 'spiritual' ground of potentiality.

Which came first? The chicken or the egg? – Question your beliefs, your thought patterns, and your 'idea' of what respect is.

Steph Thomson

I would not like limiting myself to a Vegan diet. Got to put that out there. I believe food is one of the great pleasures of life and I would just get fed up of a life of denial and guilt with every meal. Yes you can get alternatives but it's not the same, personally. Also we have evolved as meat eaters so it is natural to me genetically. I did go vegetarian for a while but fell off the wagon.

A Vegan diet is not varied enough for my personal tastes, and I see nothing wrong with eating other animal products as long as the animals well being is maintained . I do however believe in a good standard of living and a quick and 'humane' slaughter method. (I realise that this is very conflicted and I do change my mind all the time about it'). However, God in the bible says 'kill and eat' so maybe he gives us animals as a gift and to nourish us – what I mean is, the spiritual reason not to eat meat doesn't apply to me as a Christian. Jesus ate fish and Jesus was the Son of God, according to my belief.

I think basically that a high quality standard of life and care, and as quick a death as possible makes meat eating okay for me. I am actually an area rep for 'compassion in world farming'. I am open to debate about this if anyone wishes, but will not tolerate rudeness sarcasm or guilt tripping. Apart from anything else it weakens your stance.

While in the moment of being murdered, an animal is in a state of fear, uncertainty, and extreme frustration. These aspects are 'negative' energy: this negative energy remains in the physical body or 'shell' of the animal after the 'passing of spirit'. So, obviously that negative energy is now part of the meat that humans consume. If you eat meat, you are 'absorbing' this negative energy. It becomes part of you; you are what you eat indeed! It is of no surprise that humans develop cancers, heart disease, or any other physical problem! The negative energy causes an upset to the system. Obviously, with some folks, they develop physical problems through genetic 'pass-downs', but how did their family members 'of old' develop these problems? Food for thought?

I do not eat the flesh of any being;
I do not eat the natural 'by-product' derived from any being.
I do not wear wool, leather, or fur;
An animal's coat is exactly what this sentence implies –
It is the animal's coat!
I too was 'brainwashed' into the 'notion' of the illusion:
Animals are just 'animals' –
There for consumption, there for 'using'.
I purposely slipped out of the matrix,
Slipped out of a manipulated dream.
I think for myself –
You think you think for yourself:
There is a huge difference in scenarios.

Jonathan James

Andrew has asked his meat eating friends a few simple questions for his new Vegan book, so I thought he deserved a more in depth answer from me than just a simple Facebook response. His first question is, "Why are you consuming animal produce, when 'plant' alternatives are available?" The answer is simply, I have never tasted plant alternatives that taste as good as the real thing. It´s an answer to the question but to be more enlightening on what to the readers may seem a cold hearted and selfish statement, I have to dig into the theory of why I believe that´s ok.

Firstly Andrew has stated on many occasions that eating animals is effectively eating their very souls. Scientists would laugh at the notion but neither Andrew nor I are scientists, and both of us believe in souls. I too believe animals have souls. The difference is – I also believe that plants and even the planet itself have a soul. Therefore if I was to take soul consumption into consideration, I'd starve to death. Just because something is furry and has eyes doesn't place it on a level above everything else in my eyes.

Next, I have always believed Veganism is a product of our own privileged backgrounds. Andrew once released a statistic on the huge number of non-Vegans in the world and what arse-holes they are, until I raised the point that many in poorer countries are too busy trying to fight for survival, rather than where the next batch of Quorn mince is coming from. I believe that if the Vegans in this country were to live in poorer conditions, they simply wouldn't be Vegan. It´s a position of luxury. I certainly know in my heart that if I was starving to death I'd eat anything that did or didn't move, so what's the point of someone like me being Vegan? I'd be a hypocritical liar.

Thirdly and connected with the above, I don't believe the arguments of Veganism hold water. As an example of this, I asked a question that popped into my head one day. I asked, "As crude oil is a product of animal matter, should Vegans not use electricity, cook with gas or drive cars?" The first response suggested that it was fine because the animals died of natural causes. This suggests that the idea of not eating unfertilised eggs or drinking milk is nonsense, as they were never alive to begin with. Secondly, it means Vegans CAN eat meat should the animal have died naturally. I'm pretty sure that's not the position of most Vegans.

Andrew then stated that all Vegans 'sometimes' consume meat by accident, and do the best they can, and that they sometimes eat animal matter unknowingly. Trouble is, he and any Vegan reading this book now know this book was created through energy burned from animal matter. You can live without a bacon butty but can't live without your WIFI huh?

I wouldn't mind the above if Vegans weren't so 'holier than thou' preachy, but the fact is you've chosen a level of life that you're comfortable with and wouldn't sacrifice anything more. Why do you get to choose the level? Aren't you just making your opinions fit your lives just to give yourself a false feeling of goodness? It's kind of like new age Christians who say the bit about gays being an abomination should be ignored. You either believe in your faith or you don't.

To me, the only group that has any reason to crow are the people who follow fruitarianism and that's only if they built their house from dead trees and their energy is solar only. Other than that everyone should shut the hell up and live their lives.

At least I'm honest. I know I have no intention of living a life that pure, I don't have the time. That doesn't mean you should just freely eat anything. I still don't understand, for example, why battery hen farming is legal. But in my eyes, dead eggs born from a chicken who's had a good life is not a problem and never will be. Humanely killing an animal in my eyes is not different to uprooting a carrot – but only in my eyes.

Finally, if meat eaters are bad, then are all lions arse-holes? I've never seen a Lion kill an animal in a humane way ever.

The only reason I can seriously see for not eating meat is either you don't like it or you're intolerant to it. For example, I hate the texture of pears so I don't eat them. I'm not running around telling everyone how sick it is to eat pears though. I'm also semi lactose intolerant, so I tend to drink almond milk or leave it out completely.

So in answer to your second question Andrew, no, I have no intention to go Vegan and for all the reasons listed above.

What the Hell are they doing?

Alrighty then! 'Has the world gone stark raving mad?' – YES! It certainly has, I'm afraid. On a global scale, animal cruelty is tremendously frightening: dog fighting, bull fighting, seal hunting, skinning cats and dogs, bestiality – the list is endless!

We live in a twisted society it seems; the world is seemingly at war with itself. The collective consciousness has been poisoned by highly negative energies, energies that have made humanity numb, selfish, cruel, and ignorant – Uncompassionate is the main word here: the uncaring abuse of our fellow innocent creatures. 'What the hell are they doing?' Let us take a look at these atrocities; let us examine the mentalities behind such monstrosities:

Dog fighting:

Man's best friend, the loyal servant, who gives unconditional love to its owner. Dependable, reliable, and 'part of the family' – we all love dogs, well, most of us do! Once again, the minority creates a 'disturbance in the force'! In this particular problem, it is the breeding and fighting of dogs for financial gain.

Dog fighting is illegal in most parts of the world, but it still carries on in secret locations, this criminal activity is an underground affair, causing pain, suffering, and extreme violence to the overly trained animal. Dogs are often trained on treadmills, fed raw meat, and some owners have been known to bite their own dogs violently, to create aggression in their 'fighting beast'.

These bloodthirsty dog breeders, who enter their potential champions into the ring, have no compassion for animals, they are sick individuals – train, fight, injure, kill, blood, money: blood-money! One of the main types of dogs used in dog fighting is the American Pit Bull Terrier, although many types of breeds are used around the world.

There is big money to be made in dog fighting, but, as with any other form of gambling, it is hard to control from the outside. The 'so called' sport is obviously difficult to completely abolish, because of the financial interest involved. What a sad world we live in! Where grown men abuse animals in the name of the Dollar, the Pound, or whatever the hell currency you operate in.

Besides rigorous treadmill training, dogs are often starved before a fight, to make them bloodthirsty, 'hungry for the kill', and aggressive. Other small animals are sometimes used as bait to initiate the fight in the fighting pit. There are always stories about missing dogs and cats, that may have been stolen to be used as dog fighting bait. Peoples pets stolen to be ripped apart by badly trained, bloodthirsty dogs – sad, but true!

What happens to the losing dog in this horrendous blood-sport? Well, the dog may die of multiple injuries during the match, or may survive the ordeal, and live to recover for another fight – although sometimes, the owner will destroy the dog, if the dog is failing in the aftermath of the fight.

A disgrace to humanity, an embarrassment to the collective consciousness – dog breeders/dog fighters have a lot to answer for! My name is Andrew J Jones – I am a voice for the voiceless. VEGAN POWER!

Bull fighting:

Does it seem so innocent and sporting? A 'pastime' that has been carried out for hundreds of years; a crowd pleasing activity that creates *roars* and at times *abusive* behaviour from the crowd. Bullfighting – thousands of bulls are slaughtered in the ring every year. A barbaric act of 'bullying' really speaking!

They are 'manipulated' and beaten to a certain extent, before they even enter the ring. Their horns are shaven, to create an 'imbalance' in their stature; petroleum jelly is rubbed into their eyes, so to blur their vision. What chance do they have? The fights are held in Spain and other countries, and have a reputation as a 'glorious event'. The crowds cheer, boo, and even throw cans at the injured or dying bull – charming isn't it?

The reason the bull is angry is not because it is an 'aggressive' animal, it is because of the torture and misery it has experienced in the previous two days: newspapers stuffed into his ears, cotton rammed up his nose, a needle is put into his genitals – all to 'disillusion' the animal. By the time the bull actually comes out into the ring, it is a 'broken soul', weakened by the torture and abusive behavioural activities from the 'bullfighting team'. These are sick individuals who 'torment' these poor creatures; they have no compassion for animals whatsoever.

The bull is kept in a dark box for a couple of days, then when let loose, he obviously runs for the 'light' – but, he is 'unaware' of his terrible fate. The event is supposed to last about twenty minutes, but could be longer or shorter, depending on the state of the 'already-tortured' bull. The event begins when men on horseback (*picadors*) are put into the ring with the bull to 'exhaust' the poor animal. They then use a weapon known as a *pica,* which is about six to eight inches long, and cut into the bull's neck muscles – with the aim of drawing as much blood as possible (to weaken the animal even more!).

Then the *assistant matadors* come in and with their *banderillas* (sharp, harpoon pointed sticks), and further 'humiliate' and injure the bull, before the main *matador* makes his entrance. By now, obviously, the bull is on it's last legs: tired, weak, out of breath, and humiliated beyond belief. The *matador* then attempts to 'provoke' a few charges from the tired animal before finally killing the bull with his sword. If he misses, an *executioner* is 'called in' to finish the bull off.

If the crowd are happy with the *matador,* the bull's ears and tail are cut off – and believe it or not, they are used as 'trophies'!

Just another example of the twisted mentality of the 'dark side' of the collective consciousness. Animal abuse at its extreme level! Although *all* animal abuse is extreme.

Seal hunting:

Hundreds of thousands of baby seals are slaughtered every year in Canada. Apparently, the ninety seven percent of harp seals which are killed are under the age of three. 'Sealing' is carried out by fishermen in the 'off-season', and *The Canadian Marine Mammal Regulations* allow the fishermen to kill the seals with wooden clubs, hakapiks (ice-pick clubs), and guns. The baby seals are shot or repeatedly 'clubbed' during the kill – are these guys real?

Seals are often shot from a distance, and are wounded before their violent death awaits them. They are murdered and skinned to 'supply' the fur trade; although, some are actually still conscious while being skinned. There is no market for their flesh/meat, so their actual bodies are left to rot in the ice.

This is the 'sick' world we live in folks! A world where 'compassion' is a just a word, just a *'so what!'* We need to 'examine' our hearts and minds; we need to 'spread the word' on animal cruelty – it is not going to 'go away' by itself! The Canadian government not only allows these atrocities to continue, but actually funds the seal hunts with 'financial assistance' – DISGRACEFUL! Killing babies is an 'activity'.... I will say no more....

The Chinese fur industry:

China is the world's largest exporter in fur; there are no 'penalties' for animal abuse on these fur farms. Uncaring and ruthless, these people have no compassion for animals. Dogs, cats, foxes, rabbits, and many other animals are used and abused in this horrendous trade. Huddled into wire cages, unprotected from natures elements, these poor souls endure the 'harshest' of living conditions.

Before the 'skinning' takes place, they are 'grabbed' from their cages, thrown to the floor, and repeatedly beaten into surrender. Once again we see the 'disturbance' in the collective consciousness: these people are 'sick'! How can you possibly beat, murder, use, abuse, and manipulate one of God's defenceless creatures? Karma will take it's course: what goes around comes around!

Many of these animals are still conscious while the skinning is being 'executed' – can you imagine the pain and the fear involved here? What a terrible way to end someone's life. I have seen videos on the internet of these terrible experiences of *Hell* – the graphic imagery certainly sticks in your mind, although I do not view these videos on a regular basis. I know what goes on; there is no need for me to watch multiple 'cruel' animal abuse videos. I think people should at some point though, because you will not find this kind of 'truth' on the S*ix o' Clock*

News. It leaves an 'imprint on your brain', a 'kick up the ass', to remind you that life is not all 'blue skies and sunshine': a tremendous amount of violence is being carried out on the animal kingdom and obviously – the human condition.

To see an animal violently shake and struggle while being skinned, while the killer/murderer has his/her foot on its neck is a viewing experience to behold. What the hell is going through these 'sick' minds, as they are murdering a poor defenceless 'child of God'? Just like the hunting of the seal, after they are skinned, their body is thrown on top of a pile of other murdered 'beings' – with some actually still breathing! Of course they slowly 'fade away', but have experienced 'Hell on Earth'.

Bestiality:

There is 'sick', and there is SICK! What is 'bestiality'? It is humans having sex with animals. What possesses a person to actually do this? What 'frame of mind' does it take to be this 'twisted' in behavioural patterns? Is it an illness? – It is certainly a serious condition of a 'disturbed' mind. It does happen though; this behaviour is carried out by, as I have said 'disturbed' people. I think we shall leave this topic 'stand as it stands'. It really is 'self explanatory' (in this paragraph written...).

You don't drink milk?

The dairy industry: the manipulation and abuse of sentient beings – for their milk. Now, milk is for the mothers young; milk is for the mothers young! Shall I repeat it again? It is not for the 'feeding' of another species – namely the 'human'. Just like the female human, a cow carries her babies for nine months; they then 'lactate' to feed their young. Through genetic manipulation, they produce up to twelve times more milk than is necessary to feed their calves.

Most new born calves are 'stolen' from their mothers within the first twelve hours. An incredible twenty one million calves are slaughtered each year for veal or cheap beef – what a 'saddening' statistic. What is veal? The flesh of a young calf, used as food. Veal calves are confined into 'Veal crates' – Restricted in movement, so that their 'meat' is more tender – They are slaughtered at sixteen weeks.

Most calves are fed a commercial 'powdered' milk replacer;
The Females become dairy machines,
The Males are raised for 'meat' –
'How 'charming' is this particular story?'
Most Male calves are killed for beef,
While some are thrown into the 'Veal' industry.
'A pint of milk please!'

Dairy cows are artificially inseminated, and the continuous cycle of forced pregnancy takes it toll on the 'over-worked' being. After the birth of their calves, cows are then 'hooked up' to milking machines. This is 'rape': this is 'abuse'! An unnatural process to feed the greed of the human. By the age of four or five, their tired bodies can not produce the 'goods' like they used to, so they are sent to the slaughterhouse.

The industry itself promotes the 'white stuff' as healthy and full of nutritional goodness – of course it does! It is a business! A big business at that. Adverts with dancing cows: everything all 'happy and sunny' – it is really sickening to be honest!

'A pint of milk?'
Not today, thank you!
'The white stuff' –
Dead somatic cells in every glass!
'Pus' – to you and I.
....and the cow jumped over the moon!

A cow's lifespan is around the twenty five year mark, unless, in most cases, the 'greedy' dairy industry gets their hands on these beautiful beings – in which (like I mentioned earlier) they killed after four to five years.

Milk, cheese, ice-cream – if your kitchen is full of these items, you may want to question your beliefs and values. Animals are suffering in the name of your ignorance and greed. There are plenty of 'alternative' foods to dairy; there is no need to 'rape' and abuse our fellow creatures to feed our bodies. I have been Vegan for twenty three years – I am fine! I certainly do not starve. I became a good cook within these twenty three years: I make cakes, biscuits, curries, soups – you name it!

Angela R Stephens

"Just an animal"

I have always been an animal lover. Even as a child I was trying to help baby birds, bunnies and pretty much anything that needed my help. As I got older and became more aware of the atrocities that animals have to endure, my passion to help them became even stronger. I describe it as a blessing and a curse. It's not easy to feel their pain so deeply. I share emails and Facebook posts all over the country trying to help animals in need. I have so many people say to me "how can you stand seeing those pictures?" or "you know you can't help them all". My response to that is if everyone turned to a blind eye to the problem, then nothing would ever get accomplished. Yes it's heartbreaking, but if I can save just one, then I've done something to help, and if everyone did something, the problem wouldn't be so overwhelming.

One of my favourite quotes is by Albert Schweitzer "Think occasionally of the suffering of which you spare yourself the site". This statement best sums up my feelings on animal abuse. I believe that to be the attitude of most of the general population when it comes to "unpleasant" topics such as animal abuse and neglect. Most don't realize the horrific state of animal welfare in this country. The phrase "it's just an animal" to me is just like saying "it's just a child". Animals are intelligent, sensitive and share many of the same emotions as humans do. Not only can they suffer, they do every day all over the world.

An estimated 2.7 million animals die each year in shelters. That's one every 13 seconds. Animals are surrendered to the animal shelter for many ridiculous excuses: not enough time, suddenly allergic, just had a baby, going on vacation, moving and I can't take, health problems, can't afford.

Many people are reluctant to spay or neuter their pets and even feel it's not necessary. They have no idea how important it is or realize the impact it will have if they don't. Reasons to spay/neuter your cat or dog: They make better, friendlier companions; they are less likely to roam/run away/fight or bite. They are also less likely to develop certain types of cancers. No heat cycles and reduces the urge to mark territory. Bottom line, there is NO good reason to NOT spay and neuter your pet.

An un-spayed dog, her mate and her puppies if not ever spayed or neutered can produce in: 1 year – 16 litters, 2 years – 128 litters, 3 years – 512 litters, 4 years – 2,048 litters, 5 years – 12,288 litters, 6 years – 67,000 litters

An un-spayed cat, her mate and her puppies if not ever spayed or neutered can produce in: 1 year – 12 litters, 2 years – 67 litters, 3 years – 376 litters, 4 years – 2,107 litters, 5 years – 11,801 litters, 6 years – 66,088 litters

That's a staggering amount of animals to find a good and responsible home for, and believe me there isn't nearly enough of suitable homes to offset those numbers.

Did you know that only 1 out of 10 dogs born and 1 out of 12 cats born ever find a permanent home? Do not buy dogs from breeders, pet shops, or puppy mills which are all adding to the overpopulation problem of animals, and facilitating more neglect and abuse. There are beautiful, intelligent animals at your local shelter that are just waiting for a home, and will die due to lack of space. Shelter animals are not "broken" or "damaged". They are there only because of irresponsible and selfish owners.

It's bad enough that you have to be concerned with animal abuse and neglect in your own community, but immorality at animal shelters is not uncommon. What few animal abuse laws we have are rarely enforced, and the punishment is pitifully insufficient. Then there's animal testing, dog fighting, farm animals forced to live in crates, and the list goes on and on. Never give your pet away or put on sites like Craigslist. People with bad intentions often use this to get animals for testing or dog fighting.

Most importantly you should spay and neuter every pet you have, and report any animal abuse/neglect that you encounter. Donate to your local animal shelter or rescue instead of large animal welfare organizations, because more of the money goes to the animals. If you can't adopt, you can foster or sponsor an animal in need. Just get involved and educate yourself to what's happening out there.

I would like to close with another quote that I like that sums up my feeling about animal rescue, "I said somebody should do something about that, then I realized that I am that somebody" by Lily Tomlin. Everyone can do something, what will YOU do?

Mary Ann Coffey

Why are we Vegans? Why are we thinking different from the 'norm'? Are we still healthy? Why are we trying to better the world? Why are we 'sniggered at' for just having free will? – Questions that make people think …
People are changing 'slowly but surely' on their vision of how they see of food. People are understanding the levels of natural food; it is ethically and nutritionally 'righteous', and appealing to the eye. People are evolving, wanting the best for their bodies, wanting the 'truth' of what goes into their bodies, and how it effects them on a long term basis.

People hate losing loved ones through bad choice in diet, and they feel that through searching ones 'truth', they will find never ending depth to what really goes on, and that 'truth' will lead them to compassion. People will want a better lifestyle through a better world, and attached to that will be a cleansing of the mind, which will take them through many transitions and acceptance.

However, acceptance is never an easy transition to move through, but can be mastered by wanting change. Have you ever wanted something so bad, that when you have it, it appears to be better than you originally expected? How can you turn back? Why would you want to? The road gets challenging, but with the 'transitions', you have passed through that inner strength, and that becomes 'super strength'; every suffering of change will then become your 'extra strength' – energy within energy! You are what you eat: so be who you want to be!

The Compassionate Mind

No milk, no eggs, no meat, no honey;
No leather, no cheese, no way!
All beings are equal;
In essence, in thought, in existence.
It was man who decided that he should rule over beast...

Mass murder:
The slaughtering of poor defenceless beings:
All in the name of greed, religion, ignorance, and the unwillingness to change.
The uneducated must be educated;
We must bring back the balance of the compassionate mind.

Do animals have consciousness?
Do they have a soul?
Are they 'just there', but for the grace of God?
The notion of animation...puzzling in hazy wavelengths.
Surely, they have consciousness...

How can they do that?
How can someone develop a frame of mind to torture, to manipulate, to kill?
I am ashamed to be human at times:
The greedy, selfish, ignorant human.

Hell on earth:
Animal testing, seal hunting, fox hunting;

Bull fighting, the Chinese fur trade, bestiality...
Dog fighting, rabbiting, fishing;
Guns, knives, traps, rods, bloodthirsty hounds...
The innocent suffer, while the human carelessly grins.

Vegan Power!
The voice for the voiceless;
The compassionate mind,
The light at the end of the tunnel.
The Vegan vibrations are rising;
The 'evolution of mind' is about to take one giant step.
We are at the heart of the collective consciousness:
Praying, educating, rescuing, and creating a better world for
our children and our fellow creatures of the Earth.

You are what you eat

Unlike most Vegan books, my last 'Vegan' work – 'The Vegan Vibrations' hardly mentioned the topic of nutritional values and the health benefits of Veganism. That is because my books on Veganism are examining the 'ethical' and 'spiritual' aspects of Veganism. There are plenty of Vegan cookbooks, and books on nutrition out there – some good ones too!

I will however, briefly 'go through' the basics of Vegan food, and how the 'alternative' lifestyle is beneficial to our health. First and foremost, I must explain the most important factor here – energy!

At the point of slaughter, an animal has fear, confusion, heartache, and misery flowing through its body – all those aspects are *negative* energies. I mean, can you imagine 'waiting in line' to be killed? Observing your fellow creatures enduring such an horrific death – the smell of fresh blood, the cries of pain, the energies of 'fear' in the air. Don't forget animals communicate using their 'energy senses'. The *negativity* from the slaughtering process remains in the body, even after the spirit has passed on. If you consume meat, you are also 'absorbing' that *negativity*.

The same principle applies to milk or dairy: the confined and restricted conditions of living, and the manipulation of the 'over-production' of cows milk, produces negative energies – derived from the 'frustration' of being 'exploited' – and yes! Cows are exploited. Eggs? I have already explained the specifics of the 'Egg'. Is there negative energy in an 'unfertilized' egg? Probably! If only out of the 'ethics' of the whole thing. An egg is the start of a physical life – when fertilized. I really can not see there being an abundance of 'balanced' energy in an hard boiled egg.

Okay! Let us carry on – Veganism: the 'abstaining' from *all* animal produce. Anything 'derived' from animals is a big *no no!* In its values, and in its essence, Veganism is against the 'exploitation' of all beings – whether it be for clothing, food, sport, or any other 'manipulation' of an aspect of consciousness.

Obviously, the Vegan diet is a 'plant based' diet: fruits, vegetables, grains, seeds, nuts, beans, and pulses. Some of which can be eaten in their 'raw' form or cooked in some fashion to create 'whatever you desire'! – cakes, biscuits, soups, curries – the list is endless!

There are so many items *suitable for Vegans* in major and minor supermarkets, that in these 'modern times', it is pretty much easy to 'pick up' Vegan foods. It is a healthier lifestyle, I believe – and for me personally, my theory of the 'negativity' within the meat and milk 'holds ground'. It is of no wonder why people get diseases, cancers, and the like – that 'negativity' is bad for ya!
VEGAN POWER!

VEGAN POWER!

The Great Spirit's Prayer
(Reprinted from 'Prayers, Blessings, and One for the Road')

Oh Great Spirit, Almighty creator of all that has been, all there is, and all that will be –
Give us your strength, so we may rise into the comfort of the Sun;
Give us your love, so we may sleep in peaceful dreams, and awake in sunlit bliss.
May we individually and collectively seek, and find true enlightenment –
Through Prayer, Faith, Respect, and Understanding.
With an open minded view of reality, we awake each day to the beat of your heart, and to the vision of the new day.
Our hearts dwell within the Kingdom of Heaven;
Our Faith is in your gentle hands.
In the name of Infinite Love –
We are your children, your dreams, your loyal servants.
We ask of you – Guidance,
We ask of you – Words of wisdom,
And last, but not least: we ask of you – love.

Other works by Andrew J Jones:

DREAMS FROM THE MIDNIGHT SUN
PRAYERS, BLESSINGS, AND ONE FOR THE ROAD
FAITH
HELLO IT'S THE BIGMAN
THE VEGAN VIBRATIONS
FREEDOM OF THOUGHT

Printed in Great Britain
by Amazon